Butterfly

Inspirational & Motivational Story telling

Book One

Transformation of a life

Author
Eliane Mezher

Published by

EM School

Lebanon, Zalka, Saideh Street,

Mezher Bldg, 1st Floor

Copyright 2019, Eliane Mezher

Cover photo: Aaron Burden
www.unsplash.com

All rights reserved by Eliane Mezher, and content may not be reproduced, downloaded, disseminated, published, or transferred in any form or by any means, without permission in writing from the copyright owner.

Contents

Introduction	Transformation of a life	05
Chapter One	Childhood	09
Chapter Two	Adulthood	15
Chapter Three	Healing	21
Chapter Four	New Life	25
Chapter Five	Career	29
Chapter Six	Setbacks	35
Chapter Seven	Forever Forward	41
Chapter Eight	Focus	45
Chapter Nine	Cool Aunt	51
Chapter Ten	Gratitude	55

Introduction

"Imagination is more important than knowledge. Knowledge is limited. Imagination encircles the world."

Albert Einstein

We all have dreams.

We all have to search deep down our souls to draw the faith and strength necessary to make a change in our lives.

We are all the same yet very unique, our similitude lying in the uniqueness of our missions on earth.

All the research that I have done and all the books that I have read have made me into the dreamer that I am today. I gradually became aware of an inner energy in me so powerful that it could reach other people and impact their lives. It all started with changes that I brought upon myself. It all started the moment I asked myself: "What is it that I really want from my life?"

As the year 2020 approaches, I am fully convinced that now is the right time to share my story. In doing so, I hope to inspire people and encourage them to turn a crippling pain into a fortunate experience driven by ambition and shrouded in success.

My mission is to guide people on their path to freedom from any obstacles and destructive habits that might impede their progress.

How I long to convince them to take off the masks behind which they are hiding their true selves!

This is my story, a journey of self-discovery.

Childhood

"Being a family means you are a part of something very wonderful. It means you will love and be loved for the rest of your life."

Lisa Weed

When I look back at my childhood and think about my parents, I realize that they were never truly aware of all the precious moments passing them by. Having been raised in a strict, unforgiving society, I am fairly certain that they are not fully conscious of the reason they got married and why they decided to have children.

Their decisions were automated by pre-set rules that, once followed, rewarded them with a good standing among their peers. In that case, how could they become mindful and open-minded, understanding parents?

When I visualize over this issue and wonder why I could never really bond with them, I understand that their own upbringing is the reason why I could never feel truly accepted and loved by them.

They could not look past any of my shortcomings and, instead of treasuring the love and joy that I had in me, they chose to break me. How many times did I hear: "You're nothing."; "You will never succeed."; "You are but a cross-eyed child with thick glasses and a short sight." There were no limits to the creativity of the bullying that they inflicted upon me. So much energy did they invest in judging and punishing me that they forgot to love and support me in between.

I was maybe young, but I was neither deaf nor blind to the influence that my grandmother had on them and how she relentlessly tried to convince them that providing me with an education would prove useless and a waste of money.

I envied other children whose grandmothers would spoil and protect them. Mine seemed to jump at any chance to abuse me and the weight of her words crushed my soul.

Going to school was not a stroll in the park either. Teachers and administrators play a major role in creating a positive and safe environment for young students. Going to school should feel like a happy experience and children should look forward to learning.

It is up to the teachers to create a world where learning through love, patience and logic is promoted.

Sadly, I can only remember how, as a child, I felt dread at the mere idea of going to school. Fear, sadness and tears were my daily bread.

Administrators failed to see the neglect that I endured and the bullying that I was subjected to because of my thick glasses and my crossed-eyes.

Having crossed-eyes meant that I found it difficult to read properly. Instead of helping me, teachers would punish me and chastise me physically. They told me I was a hopeless loser in front of other students.

I was also made to stand in a corner in front of everyone and that only added to my humiliation.

Needless to say, my schoolmates had no mercy on me either, as children, in their naïveté, can be even crueler than adults.

I hated my life. I remember trying at all costs to avoid going to school and would hide in the basement when I heard the bus coming to pick me up in the morning.

In my plight, I found nobody to turn to. A loving relative, a grandmother, an aunt, an uncle or a cousin, capable of creating a positive relationship with me, could have compensated the missing love of a parent, in a way or another, or so one would expect.

However, my relatives abused me both emotionally and physically and never showed me any support or love. I was criticized, degraded and marginalized and as a result I chose to push them away. My cousins were not allowed to play with me because of my academic failures.

I was bullied emotionally by my cousin. Whenever a boy would approach me, my cousin would say: "Don't think you are pretty; you are blind." I therefore used to try to avoid my extended family at all costs.

How I longed, to no avail, for love, support and a healing embrace from a relative. They would neither love nor embrace me and I was left helpless.

As I grew up, the pain of being rejected by the people who are supposed to love and cherish me unconditionally became all too familiar. The results were to be expected: aggressive behavior and a series of tantrums, such as breaking glasses and plates in the basement and injuring myself in a desperate bid for attention.

A young adult is shaped by the predominant culture in the environment that he evolves in. In most cases, self-denial prevails. I kept my mask on and held tight to it in an attempt to hide my past and my fears. I concealed my scars, my regrets and all my dreams. I couldn't let anyone see the broken person that I was. One can only imagine the stress and the aftermath of such conflicted feelings; I was always sick, weak, and burning up with fever and an infection in my bronchial tubes made my breathing laborious. I was so tired and overwhelmed that I kept wishing for death to come and release me from my grief and loneliness.

As vicious circles go, I unwittingly poisoned my life with temper tantrums and overreactions that shattered all of my relationships, even with people who cared for me.

As a child, I needed my parents' emotional support more than ever. I was hoping my parents would be able to help me discover any talents or hobbies that I might have. Deep inside, I knew that I was gifted and I did not want my talent to go to waste as I desperately wanted to impress my parents by exceeding all expectations, I kept challenging myself to tackle new hobbies. However, having failed to obtain the support of my parents and being determined not to lose any given opportunity to thrive, I decided to channel the signals that I received from my senses as pain, limitation and exhaustion and turned this energy into relentless effort to maximize my potential. I started focusing on my studies, regardless of my grades. I expressed myself through drawing, painting and sculpting creations out of my imagination. I soothed myself by playing the piano or riding a bike or swimming.

Adulthood

"The body grows slowly and steadily but the soul grows by leaps and bounds. It may come to its full stature in an hour."

L.M. Montgomery

As a young adult, having barely made it through school, I was lost and exhausted from the effort it took me to graduate. I still couldn't manage to communicate with my parents. Having looked forward to going to college and starting a new life, I was faced with the strict refusal of my parents who wanted me to stay at home and help my mother instead of "wasting my father's money", as they so obtusely put it.

However, this time, I stood my ground. I stepped in and overruled the verdict. I decided to join a public university and pursue my education in order to transition into the future and embrace every possible career opportunity, thus propelling myself toward my independence.

During that time, I was beautiful and sexy and I had secret admirers. My first adult relationship, which occurred when I was twenty seven years old, was a long one, but what I learned from it is what I didn't want to deal with in relationships and it took a lot of heartache to understand that. With it being my first love story, I had no previous experience to compare it to.

Looking back on that time, what I thought was normal was, on many levels, disrespect and emotional and physical abuse and material theft. It is true as they say, though: "Sometimes we need to experience what doesn't work in order to know what does."

I take the opportunity here to say that what happens to children is definitely a determining factor in the attachment pattern that is carried into adult relationships. Trauma hugely influences attachment. Growing up happy, healthy, and in stable homes where caregivers are emotionally available and responsive to children's needs results in stable relationships and healthy attachment abilities.

Experiencing persistent neglect or abuse inevitably leads to developing a fearful-avoidant or disorganized-disoriented attachment pattern. Relationships are a mirror of these early experiences which either instill in us bad habits or break harmful cycles or even give us a whole new set of guidelines on how to approach love. I believe my childhood experience had a big influence on the relationship that I chose to remain in for so long despite its abusive basis.

With time, I found solace in prayer. Whenever I felt lost or down, a nearby monastery was where I could be found. I would spend hours having endless conversations with God, pleading for help and trying to find answers to all the questions that I had. How could I honor my father and mother if they were stuck in the past and hurt me so much? How could I really apply "Ask, and shall be given; seek and ye shall find; knock, and it shall be opened unto you?" to my daily life? How could I forgive others and myself to cleanse away all the bitterness? What did: "Children, obey your parents in the Lord, for this is right." mean? I struggled a lot to understand who God really was. I grew up a broken, empty, unfulfilled and unhappy child.

One day I tearfully implored the Holy Spirit to come to me in my dreams to help me discover who God is.

Indeed, he did. In my dreams, the Holy Spirit showed me the path to follow and how I could heal my wounds and find answers to all my questions.

Despite my parents' disapproval, I clung stubbornly to my decision to get an education. I couldn't go through life without having fulfilled my full potential and could not envision my future as a submissive and dependent adult with no real purpose in life and no benefit to society. In 2003, I graduated from a public university with a bachelor's degree in accounting. I was excited and looking forward to be trained and employed at my father's company, as I hoped my determination would have changed his opinion of me. This prospective instilled in me confidence and pride.

Shockingly, in an unexpected and traumatizing turn of events, the day came when my uncle stormed into the office and fired me with my father's approval, on the grounds of indiscretion and divulgence of company secrets. When I was younger, I did not get along with my dad. He would scold me, punish me and beat me. I turned to my uncles for guidance; they pretended to love me but only contributed to the deterioration of our already shaky father-daughter relationship. They accused me of idle gossip and instead of helping me they turned against me. Even after I joined my father's business, my uncle, whom I thought I could rely on, could not separate business and family matters.

I soon realized that I was surrounded by wolves that would stop at nothing to reach their goals, even if it meant ruthlessly backstabbing each other. I was taken aback by this attitude and had a hard time understanding it. However, I did not seem to have a choice. I decided to focus on my career and found employment elsewhere. I successfully gained a ten years' experience as an "Expert Accountant and Business Administrator" in various companies in Lebanon through hard work, perseverance, determination and passion for my job. In 2011, right before I resigned from my job, I had gotten promoted to the position of financial manager. I had received rewards from the companies for which I worked. In 2005 I had been honored with a "FRED! Making a Difference in the World" award, and, in 2009, I had been recognized for Exemplary Teamwork and success in building a collaborative working relationship among colleagues.

Healing

"The wound is the place where the Light enters you."

Rumi

Resigning from my job and freeing myself from corporate rules and regulations was the best decision I ever made. After that, I challenged myself and relied on my own motivation to further my studies. My goal was clear; I just wanted to move on. I subjected myself to various treatment methods in an attempt to overcome and release stress and anger, without obtaining satisfying results.

I then delved into the world of Hypnosis and NLP and what was to happen would exceed my wildest imagination.

New Life

"No matter how hard the past is, you can always begin again."

Buddha

As I followed the programs, I could see the impact they had on me and I started looking at the world from a new angle. I slowly started discovering how the programs help to filter ideas and experiences between conscious and subconscious to facilitate access to the subconscious mind. I could see the timeline of my childhood through my subconscious. This method is a powerful tool that releases blockages and eradicates obstacles from childhood to adulthood. I was able to encourage the inner child in me to regain confidence and believe in itself. This amazing experience allowed me to regain control of my life; it morphed the fearful, sad, unhappy, insecure and aggressive child I once was into a peaceful, happy, healthy and ambitious person whose dreams know no boundaries.

The healing process of the inner child in me comforted and reassured me, and convinced me that one day I would become the woman that I wanted to be, surrounded by a wonderful family of my own. I hugged myself and gave myself all the love and support that I yearned for. I made an inner promise to never let go of myself because I am the reason that I am today.

The awakening came slowly but I finally understood that I was not the one to blame for my once painful and tragic life.

Through hypnosis and NLP, I was able to heal my wounded inner child, thus propelling myself toward a truthful understanding of success. I looked into the eyes of my inner child and reconnected with my trustfulness, honesty, loyalty, curiosity and joy. I then realized that I was born innocent and that all I needed is to feel loved, protected, supported and encouraged. This is how I was able to maximize my positive energy and soar high in the sky, as free as a bird.

As I embarked on my healing journey, I started to develop new skills and applied the "Hypnosis & NLP" program through the visualization of the core of the problem and the creation of new pictures and affirmations to support it. I felt like I wanted others to benefit from this concept as well and thus decided to venture into that field.

Career

"Today I close the door of the past, open the door to the future, take a deep breath, take a step forward and leap into a new chapter in my life."

Eliane Mezher

I did not have enough money saved but I did not let this obstacle be an excuse to keep me from my endeavor. I had a business idea and my gut instinct told me it was a good one. I made my decision, though I knew the results would be unpredictable. I leaped into it and took my first risk even though I knew it wouldn't be easy for me to recognize problems or opportunities and to make the right decisions.

I decided that I did not need a miracle, but only to follow the steps that I learnt and rely on the knowledge and experience that I had accumulated during my ten years as an "Expert Accountant & Business Administration" in various companies in Lebanon, enabling myself therefore to run my own business successfully.

I knew that embarking on this adventure by myself would be difficult but it empowered me and boosted my focus as I was now the sole responsible for keeping the business afloat. For me, the past was over.

I opened new doors for myself and I kept my gaze turned toward the future. I was deeply passionate about my field and I started pouring my heart and soul into changing the lives of others through my studies of Hypnosis & NLP. The lack of proper financing made it a lot harder for my business to take off and it took me a lot more time and effort, but I never lost my conviction that it could be done.

I meticulously followed a few steps to start up my business and I was never discouraged by the many rejections and all the badmouthing that I was subjected to on my chosen path to success. I started networking to connect with people and let them know about what I do with every given opportunity to increase my chances of the right people finding me. I also started volunteering regularly and became an active member of the education center and shadowed my trainer who taught me Hypnosis and NLP; I never missed an opportunity to participate in local events and introduce myself to people. I relentlessly held meetings with professional people who represented my target market. I relied on social media to promote my events and reached out directly to other people in my field.

With time, I benefited enormously from presenting myself in various centers in Lebanon and encouraging people to learn and experience the power of Hypnosis & NLP.

Instead of giving in to feelings of frustration and anger when I encountered obstacles, I saw beyond the roadblocks and visualized a better future. I believed that I could overcome any obstacle by working harder. I was convinced that I had the capacity to control my circumstances, and I was highly motivated to turn adversity into opportunity. I took my first step in 2013, when I set up a small practice to continue presenting myself to the world and organizing Hypnosis and NLP group sessions.

My father was an educated and intelligent person. He was strong, charismatic and influential. When I sought his help, however, he did not accept and respect my decision to start my own business. He advised me to go back to my previous job and to be employed by a company, as a regular employee position would offer me more stability and security. His traditional mentality stood in the way of him believing in my career choice and helping me.

I can only blame this attitude on the toxic environment in which he was raised and which pushed him to neither support me nor give me his trust. I could not rely on his guidance to become an independent woman. Despite his physical presence in my life, his emotional absence resonated deeply in me as I was growing up. All his comments and actions were aimed at making me feel unattractive, devalued, and unworthy. Throughout my life, I often found myself wondering about the reason behind his attitude that aimed only at belittling me.

I knew that reaching my goal wouldn't be easy once my dad simply rejected my vision and looked down on my dream. My mother, however, adopted a different stance. She stood by me and offered me encouragement and moral support when I needed it.

Her precious guidance showed me the way when I found myself at crossroads. She also played an active role in helping me establish my business as she allowed me to use an apartment in a building that she owned to set up my first office.

My optimistic attitude is what helped me achieve desired business outcome. I never ceased to educate myself and develop new skills. I brought my dream to life by asking myself positive questions aiming at setting out a range of practical processes for amplifying success in my business: "What's working well? What needs changing? What am I learning from my mistakes? Where am I going? Am I making the right decisions?" I learned how to rely on myself and I held myself accountable for the consequences of my choices and actions, and doing so mobilized me to act. I strongly believed that my setbacks and failures stemmed from a lack of effort on my part, and I willingly did whatever it took to fix things. I made a determined decision to fully believe in myself by learning from all the negative feedback that I received from the participants. Being criticized is never easy, no matter how advanced I am in my career. It's natural for me to feel upset when I receive negative remarks. However, these remarks have always been an incredible opportunity for me to show my ability to learn and grow and my endless drive to move forward and continue chasing my dreams despite adversity.

This chapter in my life taught me to become an independent woman standing firmly on my own feet, believing in myself and reconditioning my pain into serenity, wisdom and growth. Instead of being disappointed by setbacks, I gained valuable insight by exercising my mind to find solutions to pursue my path. With time and experience I grew more and more confident of the woman that I was and the type of love that I wanted, needed, and deserved; alongside the type of love I wanted, needed, and deserved to give.

Today, I am still learning what love should feel like to me, as a woman who was raised in the shadow of mixed messages and who had to suffer through her father's many mistakes, when she only expected him to protect her and love her unconditionally.

Setbacks

"Live the Life of Your Dreams

When you start living the life of your dreams, there will always be obstacles, doubters, mistakes and setbacks along the way. But with hard work, perseverance and self-belief there is no limit to what you can achieve."

Roy T. Bennett

Success did not come without many major setbacks, however. Circumstances were not my only adversary as many people that I came across stuck to me like leeches, trying to suck out of me every ounce of profit possible.

Sometimes the wrong trainer, mentor or psychologist could teach us the right lessons in our life. When I first met my mentor, I felt relief. She seemed to take genuine interest in me and treated me like she would her daughter. She encouraged me to set up my own office space and promised me a loyal partnership. I found with her comfort, guidance and love… or seemingly so.

Unfortunately, she was not true to her word, as I was soon to find out. She saw how hard I was working and how I was fighting to make my dreams come true.

Not too long passed before I realized that she was in fact taking advantage of me to serve her own interests. When her mask fell, I found out that she was an unstable person who took me for granted. She got acquainted with all my weaknesses and she promised not to leave me until I have become an independent woman who has freed herself from the toxic environment in which she had grown up. Everything she had learned about me during our hypnotherapy sessions served as a weapon for her to use against me in a bid to completely destroy my relationship with my father.

Having been convinced of setting up a business together, I turned to my mom who gave me an office space in a building that she owned. Business thrived for a while and, in January of 2014, I decided to expand the work and rent all the office space. Thus was born "Eliane Mezher Hypnotherapy and Workshops".

We agreed on decorating it appropriately and I requested a hefty loan from a bank for that purpose. My mentor already knew which ideas I had and that I was working hard to concretize them.

I was indeed a practical dreamer, always ready to take action when it helped me inch one step closer to realizing my dreams.

That is when she abandoned me mid-way to show everyone

that I was a failure. As soon as the opportunity presented itself, she left me and abused me verbally and emotionally. She used her knowledge of my weak points to her advantage. She put me down and left me drowning in debts amounting to ten thousand dollars. She wanted my father to witness my business plan failing. It was an atrocious period, during which I did not feel like getting out of bed. The gutting situation left me too depressed to go out and face the world. I put on forty kilograms. I wanted to be invisible. What happened had hit me hard and the pain was unfathomable. Despite this unpleasant experience, I decided to hang on to dear life and not give up.

I encouraged myself to go with the flow and focus on lessons learnt rather than losses endured. I needed to develop my full potential and apply it where I could benefit from it.

Springing back on my feet, I worked harder than ever and went live on TV and radio shows, promoting my business with one idea in mind: settle my loan. It was a tough period for me and the responsibility was immense. I set up meetings with doctors to present myself as a hypnotherapist and I called in new coaches to organize workshops at my center, targeting thriving startup business and new customers looking to build winning teams. What others saw as a barrier looked like an opportunity to me.

Throughout my plight, my determined optimism never wavered and my work ethic inspired and energized all the people around me. I always had in the back of my mind what I had seen that night in my dreams, when the Holy Spirit appeared to me to lighten my way. I kept my eye on the goal and monitored my progress even as the journey took unexpected twists and turns, and my natural tendency to push forward in adverse circumstances grew stronger as time went by.

I had just only begun my journey of transformation when my former mentor got wind of my success.

As expected, she made a comeback into my life in an attempt at reaping the fruits of my hard labor. On my birthday, she showed up and explained to me that she had been experimenting with shock therapy as a means of boosting my ability to rely on myself.

As they say: "Fool me once, shame on you. Fool me twice, shame on me." Once again, we became partners. It was indeed my mistake to trust her again. This time, the profits she made from my work and my name amounted to seventy thousand dollars. As she would claim when confronted about it, I did not deserve to receive a percentage of this money because I hadn't put any effort into making it, so I only managed to obtain twenty per cent of all the profit that she made. I later learned from a client that she was pretending to all my clients and students that I was only her mentally unstable secretary.

Following this episode, I made the decision to ban her from my center and called upon a trainer from the UK to replace her and dispense the hypnosis and NLP courses.

This person also made a huge profit amounting to fifteen thousand dollars within two months. As luck would have it, all the trainers and facilitators that I hired at that time tried to take advantage of my reputation and gain control of the center. Unfortunately, a lot of people around me thought they could play me for financial gains, not knowing that they would forever lose my trust and friendship.

Forever forward

"The universe doesn't give you what you ask for with your thoughts - it gives you what you demand with your actions."

Steve Maraboli

Through the ups and downs, I never ceased to aim higher. In 2016, I decided to travel to the United States of America to attend a training that would benefit me greatly. My cousin, who lived there, helped me obtain a visa and played a big role in supporting me through the challenges that I faced and on my path to become a leader in my own field.

At that time, I turned to my dad for help once again and asked him if he could lend me ten thousand dollars that would enable me to pursue my studies in the US. He, of course, denied my request on the grounds of mistrust and that constituted yet another shock for me.

I did, however, go to the bank the next day and took out a loan which got miraculously approved within forty eight hours and I was able to travel. Off I went to explore new horizons.

On the 15th of August, as the plane took off, a wave of conflicting emotions took over me. I couldn't decide whether I was heartbroken because my father had not believed in me or if I was elated because my dreams were about to come true. All in all, my trip of two weeks to the USA ended up being a great adventure during which I explored a new country and encountered many new people.

Finally, I graduated as a certified instructor in NGH and as a trainer NLP in NFNLP.

In 2017 I met my loyal partner, a medical doctor who took the school to the next level of scientific teaching. and together we changed the name of the business to "Eliane Mezher School of Hypnosis & NLP" We decided to expand the work of the school and add more trainings and workshops that would be US certified. We had a shared will to move forward to the next level of teaching and we divided our missions at the school in a way that would best reflect our qualifications as trainers.

We never ceased to accumulate knowledge and experience by sharing and training others while remaining focused on constantly learning and enriching ourselves.

Focus

"It is during our darkest moments that we must focus to see the light."

Aristotle Onassis

My vision flowed freely, and my goals never ceased to grow. I thrived to create a good environment at the school and I focused all my attention on applying new strategies and paving the way for new energy to flow and a brand new beginning.

Nowadays, my work as a managing director is primarily about managing EM School.

However, to enable me to work efficiently and effectively in those areas, having the following skillset is invaluable: Thinking strategically and constantly setting new goals, efficiently managing budgets, resolving problems and making marketing decisions and, most importantly, being lenient and open to change at all times. These skills allow me to monitor the school's progress closely and modify my strategies and goals accordingly and always make the most beneficial decisions.

In my experience, people who can challenge themselves and others and continuously strive to reach new goals are happier and healthier than those who don't.

On a daily basis, I challenge myself on the personal and professional level and I am in the process of a constant transformation. I am convinced that shortcuts would not benefit me and that I would only grow through challenge. Every time I feel like giving up, my faith in God and my belief in my own abilities help me take one more step towards my dreams.

I do not miss any opportunity to develop new skills and my willpower helps me weather the storms. As a leader, every time I face a problem, I ask myself if what I am creating, promoting and allowing is negative for the school. I need to take responsibility and identify new ways to overcome obstacles. I look at available resources and opportunities to bring about the most efficient solutions. It is my duty to promote a culture of trust and positive values at my school.

In many ways I believe that leadership, challenge, and a resilient personality are the keys to success in my life. I have a high tolerance for stress and an immense ability to sustain hard work. I push myself through every situation with robust energy and stamina, and I listen carefully and respectfully to what people are trying to communicate to me. Any misunderstanding or disagreement can be resolved, in my opinion, when people remain professional and respectful and keep an open mind.

This attitude, I believe, can only help in bettering our lives. With time, I successfully managed to get rid of all the toxic people around me and turn the school into a second home for my students. I disregarded misleading people and tuned out distracting sounds around me. With personal effort, I lead the school in a positive direction, knowing that I am the only one who knows who I truly am and what I can offer, better than anyone else. Being the curious, quick and ambitious learner that I am and being extremely passionate about what I do, I decided to break down even more obstacles, regardless of the new experiences that I might go through. I tried to take advantage of every moment that life offered me to better myself and I enjoyed the process of transformation despite the pain that it brought with it.

This kind of experience happened through applying a behavior changing technique to help myself disassociating from all the negativity surrounding me through a process of watching others and imitating their behavior without being influenced or affected.

The best way a leader can demonstrate transparency is to show vulnerability and not camouflage weaknesses.

Evaluations and feedback taught me that my business could benefit from information acquired from clients and students in terms of value and efficiency.

EM School has changed people's perspective about hypnosis and NLP. They understand now that hypnosis and NLP are tools for the participants to access the power of their subconscious mind, to release the traumas and blockages holding them back, and make changes which would enable them to move forward toward the person they wish to be.

EM School's aim is also to raise awareness about hypnosis and NLP through TV interviews, radio programs, social media and conferences. Social media helped me greatly in promoting the school in a positive light, building a great reputation and creating solid relationships with my target audience.

It also enabled me to remain in touch with customers and be aware of their positive and negative impressions. In the end, I was able to draw a thorough marketing plan which pushed me further toward my goals of success.

Cool Aunt

"Beautify your inner dialogue. Beautify your inner world with love light and compassion. Life will be beautiful."

Amit Ray

I look back in my history at the moment I cut the cord with the wrong people and environment which had caused my inner child to store all the memories that impacted me so negatively. I drew lessons from all my experiences, good and bad, and shed off the guilt that was weighing so heavily on my shoulders once

I realized that whatever had happened to me was through no fault of mine.

I am now ready to learn how to become a healthy and fantastic mother and will be giving my child the skills to rise from upsets and pave his or her way to success. Meanwhile, having seven nieces and nephews, I believe that my role as aunt is crucial but different. I must provide them all with unconditional love, security, support and a safe space in which they can be true to themselves and to me, their trustworthy aunt and godmother.

They must be able to confide in me about their lives, their worries, their friendships and relationships, and indeed they do.

As their aunt, I play a role that their parents cannot necessarily fulfill. I am their confidante and their friend. They also rely on me to provide them with solutions to their problems which will only become more serious as they age. I listen even to their most trivial stories and I keep an open mind and heart, away from judgment and all the reproaches that a parent could address to their child.

I try to help them distinguish between good and bad, right and wrong and I try to help them understand and manage their emotions and try to emphasize the idea of a safe haven they can always turn to when they find themselves alone and in need of love.

With time, I have grown certain of the fact that I am the one who is the most qualified to help them grow up in a happy, healthy and stable environment and develop a healthy attachment pattern that applies both to their personal and social lives.

Gratitude

"Gratitude makes sense of our past, brings peace for today, and creates a vision for tomorrow."

Melody Beattie

Honestly, I don't know what I could have achieved without all the people I met in my life. They taught me so much and I'm so grateful to them! Their encouragement and constant motivation pushed me to become the person that I am today and even criticism challenged me to constantly better myself.

I am inspired by people who know where they are going, who strive joyfully to accomplish their goals and are determined to accomplish what they set out to do and do it enthusiastically and with hope. I want to be like them, to get to where they have gotten, and follow in their footsteps to be among the winners. I aspire to inspire others on how to turn a deconstructive pain into constructive ambition and success.

I learnt to be mindful at work through my experiences.

This attitude improved my physical self, reduced my stress, boosted my immune system and made me more creative and innovative. I became more energetic, felt happier and was able to prioritize and complete work better.

I dedicate this book to my mom, for whose moral and financial support I'll forever be grateful. She never ceased to push me and she accompanied me on my transformation path, opening doors for me and advising me.

As I went through the darkest periods of my life, she was there to light the way.

She had always had the foresight to predict that no good would come out of my relationship with my mentor and now I do wish I had listened to her.

I am sharing with you my story today, as an example of how hope does not give up on us when we do not give up on hope. I know that we have all toiled under the weight of pain, struggle, bullying, frustration and more. Some of us pray, others lose their way.

Some stay home, others go astray; they find sanctuary in drugs, alcohol, sex or gambling, unwittingly escaping from one prison straight into the confines of another.

In other words, there comes a moment in our lives where we have to make a choice. Do we put the blame on others and watch as life goes by slowly wasted on bitterness and rancor or do we get a grip, stand tall and regain control of our lives in order to invest our power in rising from the ashes of destruction and soaring toward new dreams?

I have made my choice. I have chosen to work and overcome all the obstacles that have faced me throughout my life. I wanted physical and mental health. I was eager to have a positive impact on my physical and spiritual self. I wanted to break free from the shackles of the traditions that I was raised upon and which I knew would only pull me back. I longed to step forward and discover my true self. I have come to the conclusion that we all have three options in life: Give up, give in or give it all we've got. The path is clear; I shall keep giving my dreams all I've got, until my last breath.

When you Change your Perception, Your Life will Change.
Eliane Mezher

Made in the USA
Columbia, SC
04 June 2025

58897355R00035